A LOOK AT ANCIENT CIVILIZATIONS

ANCIENT INDIA

BY DANIEL R. FAUST

 Gareth Stevens
PUBLISHING

CRASHCOURSE

Please visit our website, www.garethstevens.com. For a free color catalog of all our high-quality books, call toll free 1-800-542-2595 or fax 1-877-542-2596.

Cataloging-in-Publication Data

Names: Faust, Daniel R.
Title: Ancient India / Daniel R. Faust.
Description: New York : Gareth Stevens Publishing, 2019. | Series: A look at ancient civilizations | Includes glossary and index.
Identifiers: LCCN ISBN 9781538231456 (pbk.) | ISBN 9781538230039 (library bound) | ISBN 9781538233252 (6 pack)
Subjects: LCSH: India--Civilization--To 1200--Juvenile literature.
Classification: LCC DS425.F385 2019 | DDC 934--dc23

First Edition

Published in 2019 by
Gareth Stevens Publishing
111 East 14th Street, Suite 349
New York, NY 10003

Designer: Reann Nye
Editor: Tayler Cole

Photo credits: Series art (writing background) mcherevan/Shutterstock.com, (map) Andrey_ Kuzmin/Shutterstock.com; cover, p. 1 Waj/Shutterstock.com; p. 5 ekler/Shutterstock.com; p. 7 Werner Forman/Universal Images Group/Getty Images; p. 9 William Dwight Whitney, Charles Rockwell Lanman/Ms Sarah Welch/Wikipedia.org ; p. 11 Probably Nurpur, Punjab Hills, Northern India/ShotgunMavericks/Wikipedia.org; p. 13 saiko3p/Shutterstock.com; p. 17 Mivr/Shutterstock.com; p. 19 Everett - Art/Shutterstock.com; p. 21 (top) PHGCOM/ Uploadalt/Wikipedia.org; p. 21 (middle, bottom) PHGCOM/World Imaging/Wikipedia.org; p. 23 BasPhoto/Shutterstock.com; p. 25 spiber.de/Shutterstock.com; p. 27 rasika108/ Shutterstock.com; p. 29 Waj/Shutterstock.com.

Printed in the United States of America

CPSIA compliance information: Batch #CW19GS: For further information contact Gareth Stevens, New York, New York at 1-800-542-2595.

CONTENTS

Words in the glossary appear in **bold** type the first time they are used in the text.

THE INDUS VALLEY CIVILIZATION

Modern India gets its name from the Indus River, one of three major rivers of the Indian **subcontinent**. Around 4000 BC, people began to farm alongside the Indus River. They built villages and raised goats, sheep, and cattle. Over time, these villages grew into larger cities.

Indus River

●←Harappa

Mohenjo-daro● **INDUS VALLEY CIVILIZATION**

Brahmaputra River

Thar Desert

Ganges River

Arabian Sea

Indian Ocean

Make the Grade

The earliest settlements were built near rivers. With lots of water nearby, farmers could grow more food to feed more people. This led to the growth of cities.

The cities built along the Indus River were part of the Indus Valley, or Harappan, civilization. These cities were very advanced for their time. They had well-planned streets, indoor bathrooms, and **sewer** systems that ran throughout the whole city.

Make the Grade

India is one of four great ancient civilizations. The other three are Egypt, China, and Mesopotamia.

Harappan city of Mohenjo-daro, 2500-2000 BC

THE VEDIC PEOPLE

The Vedic people came into the Indus River valley around 1500 BC. They brought new ways of life and beliefs. Over time, they created a new civilization. The name "Vedic" comes from the Vedas, which were the books of beliefs the people followed.

Make the Grade

Unlike the Harappans, who had lived in large cities, the Vedic people lived on farms and in small villages.

HINDUISM AND BUDDHISM

Religion was a major part of most ancient civilizations. The religion of the Vedic people changed slowly over time and became Hinduism. The main ideas of Hinduism center around the four goals of life: duty, work, **passion**, and freedom.

Make the Grade

Hindus believed that the god Brahma created Earth and everything found on Earth.

Buddhism is another major religion that began in India. Buddhism is a religion based on the teachings of a man named Siddhartha Gautama. Gautama was a prince from a kingdom in northeast India. He became the first Buddha, or "**enlightened** one."

Make the Grade

Buddhism spread throughout Asia and influenced the beliefs and ways of life of people in other countries such as China, Japan, and Korea.

13

THE CASTE SYSTEM

The caste system was a basic belief of Hinduism. It separated the people of India into four main classes based on their work and religious duty. People in the highest caste had the most **wealth** and power.

HINDU CASTE SYSTEM

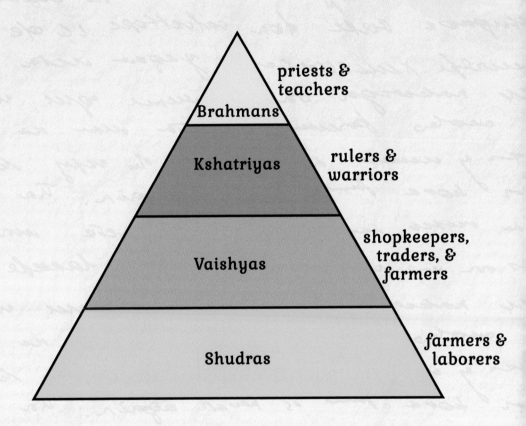

Brahmans — priests & teachers

Kshatriyas — rulers & warriors

Vaishyas — shopkeepers, traders, & farmers

Shudras — farmers & laborers

Make the Grade

People were born into a caste based on their family's wealth and power. The people of each caste could only work certain jobs and marry people of the same caste.

THE 16 KINGDOMS

Around 700 BC, 16 kingdoms began to rise in the Ganges River valley. Several of these 16 mahājanapadas (mah-HAH-jahn-ah-pah-dahs), or "great states," fought for control over the area. The state of Magadha won and grew into the greatest of the mahājanapadas.

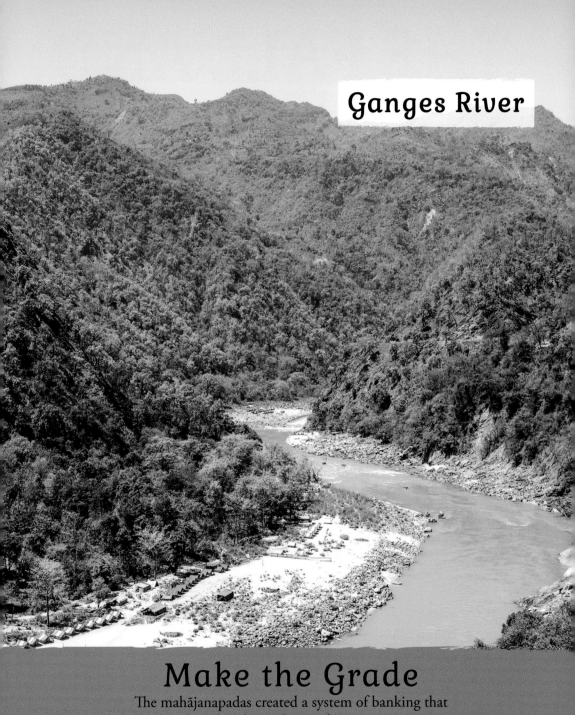

Ganges River

Make the Grade

The mahājanapadas created a system of banking that
included making silver and copper coins.

THE FALL AND RISE OF INDIA

Around 515 BC, northern India was **conquered** by the **Persian Empire**. India was **invaded** again in 327 BC by Alexander the Great. After Alexander died in 323 BC, the Mauryan Empire rose to power. This empire would soon control most of the Indian subcontinent.

Make the Grade

After the Mauryan Empire fell, India broke apart into many small kingdoms that often fought among themselves.

THE GOLDEN AGE

The rise of the Gupta Empire brought the Indian subcontinent peace and wealth. Chandra Gupta I spent money on the arts, math, and medicine. This created a golden age in Ancient India. Visitors from outside India were often amazed by this wealthy, advanced empire.

coins from the
Gupta Empire

Make the Grade

The Gupta Empire may have been founded by a member
of the second-lowest caste! Under the caste system, it was
very hard for someone from a lower caste to rise to power.

SANSKRIT

Most of what we know about ancient India comes from writings of the Vedic people. These writings are in a language called Sanskrit. Sanskrit writings include works on math and the stars, and two long poems: the *Ramayana* and the *Mahabharata*.

Sanskrit

Make the Grade

Sanskrit is one of the official languages of India. It has also **influenced** other languages throughout Southeast Asia.

INVENTIONS OF ANCIENT INDIA

Many **concepts** and inventions that are common today were created in ancient India. The concept of zero came from ancient India, as did the decimal system. Some scientists in ancient India even suggested Earth moved around the sun.

$$\sqrt{1 + \frac{4}{x^6}} \, \right)^{\frac{3}{\prime}}$$

$$= 4x^3 \left(1 + \frac{4}{x^6}\right) \sqrt{1 + }$$

$$x^3 \sqrt{1 + \frac{4}{x^6}} \qquad (4 - $$

$$\sqrt{1 + \frac{4}{x^6}} \left(4x^3 - \frac{20}{x^3}\right)\right]^{\frac{3}{\prime}}$$

Make the Grade

The concept of zero comes from Indian ways of thinking. The zero was used as a symbol for *shunya*, which means "emptiness."

$$x^7 \, \right) + \sqrt{4}$$

Around 2500 BC, the Harappans began growing cotton. The cotton cloth they made was later traded as a **luxury** good. Indigo, a bright blue dye, is also thought to come from India. The Greeks called this blue color *indikon*, which means "from India."

Make the Grade

The modern games chess and Chutes and Ladders are both based on games that were invented in ancient India.

THE GUPTA EMPIRE FALLS

After the fall of the Gupta Empire around AD 550, India once again broke apart into smaller kingdoms. These kingdoms were unable to stop Arab Muslims from coming into India from the north. India would remain under the control of other countries until the mid-twentieth century.

Taj Mahal

Make the Grade

The native people of India and the Muslim newcomers
had a hard time living with each other because of their
different religions and ways of life.

29

TIMELINE OF ANCIENT INDIA

c. 3500–2600 BC
The Harappan civilization
is established.

1500 BC
The Vedic people enter the
Indus River valley.

700 BC
The 16 mahājanapadas come
to power in northeast India;
an early form of
Hinduism appears.

c. 515 BC
The Persian Empire takes
over northern India.

500–400 BC
Buddhism spreads
throughout India.

327 BC
Alexander the Great
conquers parts of India.

c. AD 550
The Gupta Empire ends.

GLOSSARY

concept: an idea of what something is or how it works

conquer: to take by force

enlightened: having an open mind and showing a good understanding of how people should be treated

influence: to have an effect on

invade: to enter a place to take it over

luxury: something that offers more than needed and is usually more expensive

passion: a strong feeling of excitement for something or about doing something

Persian Empire: an empire in western Asia during ancient times

religion: a belief in and way of honoring a god or gods

sewer: a pipe system that is usually underground that is used to carry away water and waste matter

subcontinent: a large area of land that is a part of one of Earth's seven major landmasses (North America, South America, Europe, Asia, Africa, Australia, and Antarctica)

wealth: the value of all the money, land, and belongings that someone or something has

FOR MORE INFORMATION

BOOKS

Ali, Daud. *Ancient India*. Helotes, TX: Armadillo Children's Publishing, 2013.

Wood, Alix. *Uncovering the Culture of Ancient India*. New York, NY: PowerKids Press, 2016.

WEBSITE

Religions: Hinduism
www.bbc.co.uk/religion/religions/hinduism/
Learn more about the history, concepts, and beliefs of Hinduism.

Publisher's note to educators and parents: Our editors have carefully reviewed this website to ensure that it is suitable for students. Many websites change frequently, however, and we cannot guarantee that a site's future contents will continue to meet our high standards of quality and educational value. Be advised that students should be closely supervised whenever they access the internet.

INDEX